READING POWER

In the Ring with Sting

Michael Payan

The Rosen Publishing Group's
PowerKids Press ™
New York

To Greg and Casey...wishing you eternal love and happiness

Published in 2002 by The Rosen Publishing Group, Inc.
29 East 21st Street, New York, NY 10010

First Edition

Book Design: Michael Donnellan

Photo Credits: All photos by Colin Bowman

Payan, Michael.
In the ring with Sting / Michael Payan.
    p. cm. — (Wrestlers)
Includes bibliographical references and index.
ISBN 0-8239-6044-7
1. Sting (Wrestler), 1959—Juvenile literature. 2. Wrestlers—United States—Biography—Juvenile literature. [1. Sting (Wrestler), 1959– 2. Wrestlers.] I. Title.
GV1196.S75 P39 2002
796.812'092–dc21

                                                                00–013203

Manufactured in the United States of America

Contents

Sting is a wrestler.

Sting wears white
face paint.

Sting wears dark clothing.
Sting holds a baseball bat.

Sting has a scorpion on his wrestling tights.

11

Sting wrestles in the ring.
He jumps in the air.

Sting wrestles outside the ring, too.

Sting kicks his opponent outside the ring.

Sting is the winner. Sting yells when he wins.

When Sting is not wrestling, he meets his fans.

Glossary

fans (FANZ) People who admire an athlete or celebrity.

opponent (uh-POH-nent) A person who is on the opposite side in a game or match.

ring (RING) A square, enclosed area where wrestling matches take place.

scorpion (SKOR-pee-un) An insect with a long body and an upcurved tail that ends in a poisonous stinger.

Here is another book to read
about Sting:

*The Story of the Wrestler They Call
'Sting' (Pro Wrestling Stars)*
by Kyle Alexander
Paperback (March 2000)

To learn more about Sting, check out
these Web sites:

http://homepages.lycos.com/JenLS4L/
    lycelebrity/stingfan.html
http://members.tripod.com/
    ~Tbone101/index-4.html
www.wcw.com/2000/superstars/stin

Index

Word Count: 67

Note to Librarians, Teachers, and Parents

If reading is a challenge, Reading Power is a solution! Reading Power is perfect for readers who want high-interest subject matter at an accessible reading level. These fact-filled, photo-illustrated books are designed for readers who want straightforward vocabulary, engaging topics, and a manageable reading experience. With clear picture/text correspondence, leveled Reading Power books put the reader in charge. Now readers have the power to get the information they want and the skills they need in a user-friendly format.